Study Buddy

BIBLE STUDY GUIDE

Proverbs – Growing in Wisdom

Amber Lia

Cover Design by Alle McCloskey, Finding Eden Media, Ohio
Cover Illustration by Prixel Creative
Edited by Nate McCloskey, Finding Eden Media, Ohio
Page Design and Layout by Alle McCloskey, Finding Eden Media, Ohio

STUDY BUDDY BIBLE STUDY GUIDE: PROVERBS — GROWING IN WISDOM
Copyright © 2017 Amber Lia
Published by Mother of Knights Press
Granada Hills, CA 91344
www.motherofknights.com

Printed in the United States of America

TABLE OF CONTENTS

LETTER TO PARENTS

Hear, O Israel: The Lord our God, the Lord is one. Love the Lord your God with all your heart and with all your soul and with all your strength. These commandments that I give you today are to be on your hearts. Impress them on your children. Talk about them when you sit at home and when you walk along the road, when you lie down and when you get up. Tie them as symbols on your hands and bind them on your foreheads. Write them on the doorframes of your houses and on your gates.

Deuteronomy 6:4-9 (NIV)

Dear Parents,

The Study Buddy series is a unique resource that equips and encourages your child to study the Word of God with you beside them. Although this guide is designed for children between the ages of 7-12, it can be adjusted with a bit more guidance from you to fit the needs of younger children.

One way to use the Study Buddy Bible Study Guide is to have your child work independently on each day's material, and then go over it together when they're finished. You can also use the guide to spark a group discussion for your entire family! My own children love to review the answers in the Kid Corner and the Parent Chat sections as part of our bedtime routine. My 5-year-old recently told me his favorite part is when they all get to share!

The study should take approximately ten minutes for your child to complete. I've found this time frame allows the lesson to take root without overtaxing the child's attention span. The simplicity of the study puts the focus directly on what the Bible teaches, so feel free to explain certain terms or ideas further to aid your child's understanding. This Study Buddy Bible Study is the springboard for you to train your children about God and His plan for our lives.

You may want to begin or end your study time with prayer — keep it simple and invite the Holy Spirit to lead you both. Ask your kids if they have anything they would like you to pray about. It's my own prayer that this Bible study will be a time to enrich your own heart as you lead your child, and that the Truth will benefit you both, all the days of your lives.

With much love, ♡ *Amber*

LETTER TO KIDS

Hear, my son, and accept my words, that the years of your life may be many. I have taught you the way of wisdom; I have led you in the paths of uprightness.

Proverbs 4:10-11 (ESV)

WHO WROTE THE BOOK OF PROVERBS?

Solomon is the main author, while the final two chapters are written by Agur and King Lemuel.

WHAT IS WISDOM?

Wisdom is the ability to use good judgment and take the best course of action.

Have you ever had a problem and wondered what to do about it? By studying and writing out these verses from the book of Proverbs, you and your parents will learn how to avoid foolish mistakes! No one wants to be a fool, right?

You will also learn to live a life that is pleasing to God. Be sure to have your Bible and favorite pen or pencil out so you can copy the verse for each day. You can do this together with your parents or talk about it with them after you have completed your study for the day! Let's begin!

P.S. I recommend you use the New International Version (NIV) or English Standard Version (ESV) of the Bible for answering the questions!

With much love, ♡ *Amber*

DAY 1

TODAY'S VERSE: PROVERBS 1:7 (NIV)

The fear of the Lord is the beginning of knowledge, but fools despise wisdom and instruction.

★ COPY THE VERSE HERE:

→ BIG IDEA:

Knowing God makes us wise!

♡ KID CORNER:

1. To "fear" the Lord means to respect Him and be in awe of Him. What do we gain when we fear the Lord?

2. What do fools do?

PARENT CHAT:

Ask your mom or dad to share about a time they acted foolishly. Listen carefully to see what happened and what they should have done differently. Then it's your turn! Tell them about a time you acted wisely! What good choice did you make and what happened?

DAY 2

,,TODAY'S VERSE: PROVERBS 3:5-6 (ESV)

Trust in the Lord with all your heart,
  and do not lean on your own understanding.
In all your ways acknowledge Him,
  and He will make straight your paths.

★COPY THE VERSE HERE:

→BIG IDEA:

Always trust God, and you will be okay!

♡ KID CORNER:

1. Sometimes hard or confusing things will happen in your life. What does God want you to do at that time?

2. Look at verse 6. What does God promise He will do for you?

💬 PARENT CHAT:

Life is not always easy, and sometimes we will have to go through suffering, but we can see good things come from hard times when we trust the Lord. Together with your parents, think of a fairytale, story from a book, or example from the Bible where someone chose to do the right thing or trust in God, and things turned out well for them.

DAY 3

TODAY'S VERSE: PROVERBS 3:27 (NIV)

Do not withhold good from those to whom it is due, when it is in your power to act.

★COPY THE VERSE HERE:

BIG IDEA:

Do good to others!

♡KID CORNER:

1. Who should we not withhold good from?

2. When should we do good to others?

●PARENT CHAT:

Together with your parents, write out a list of five people you can show kindness to over the next month as you complete this study. Be specific about what you plan to do, like allowing someone at a store to go in line ahead of you or helping your teacher clean desks in your classroom!

DAY 4

TODAY'S VERSE: PROVERBS 4:23 (NIV)

Above all else, guard your heart,

for everything you do flows from it.

COPY THE VERSE HERE:

BIG IDEA:

Protect your heart!

♥KID CORNER:

1. What are you supposed to do with your heart?

2. What flows from your heart?

PARENT CHAT:

God wants us to be careful about the things we allow into our hearts so that we do not sin. Talk with your parents and ask them these questions:

- What's one way you guard your heart so you don't sin?
- What's one way you can help me guard my heart?

DAY 5

TODAY'S VERSE: PROVERBS 8:13 (NIV)

To fear the Lord is to hate evil;
    I hate pride and arrogance,
    evil behavior and perverse speech.

★ COPY THE VERSE HERE:

→ BIG IDEA:

Wise people hate evil behavior!

♡ KID CORNER:

1. Who should we have "fear" or reverence for?

2. What five things does wisdom hate?

💬 PARENT CHAT:

All of us struggle to do the right thing. God understands and loves us anyway. Share with your parents what wrong behavior you are struggling with this week. Ask them what wrong behavior they are trying to change. Take a moment to pray for each other and ask God to help you resist temptation and give you victory.

DAY 6

❞TODAY'S VERSE: PROVERBS 10:12 (NIV)

Hatred stirs up conflict,
   but love covers over all wrongs.

★COPY THE VERSE HERE:

⇥BIG IDEA:

Hateful actions lead to trouble!

♡KID CORNER:

1. What does hatred stir up?

2. What does love do?

💬PARENT CHAT:

Jesus loves you even more than your parents do! That's a lot of love! Take turns with your parents and share one thing you love about each other.

This verse tells us that love covers wrongs. That's a lot like forgiveness! Do you need to say "I'm sorry" to your parents for something you've done this week? Parents, do you need to apologize to your child, too? If so, talk about it now, and then let your love cover over the situation!

DAY 7

💬TODAY'S VERSE: PROVERBS 11:25 (NIV)

A generous person will prosper;

whoever refreshes others will be refreshed.

⭐COPY THE VERSE HERE:

⇒BIG IDEA:

We are blessed when we bless others!

♡KID CORNER:

1. What happens to the generous person?

2. What happens to the person who refreshes others?

PARENT CHAT:

Doesn't it feel good to be kind to others? What's one of the nicest things your parents ever did for you? Take a few minutes to talk about that memory with your mom or dad and remember how good it felt to receive their kindness. Now, think of a time you were generous to a friend or family member. How did it make you feel?

DAY 8

TODAY'S VERSE: PROVERBS 12:15 (NIV)

The way of fools seems right to them,
   but the wise listen to advice.

★COPY THE VERSE HERE:

BIG IDEA:

Listen to good advice!

♡KID CORNER:

1. What does a fool think about his own ideas?

2. What do wise people do?

PARENT CHAT:

Think about a current problem or challenge you have. Talk about it with your parents and ask them for advice. Be sure to listen and consider their ideas. You are on your way to being a wise young man or woman who listens to the counsel of others!

DAY 9

💬 TODAY'S VERSE: PROVERBS 17:14 (NIV)

Starting a quarrel is like breaching a dam;
    so drop the matter before a dispute breaks out.

★ COPY THE VERSE HERE:

→ BIG IDEA:

Don't start a fight!

♡KID CORNER:

1. What is starting a fight compared to in this verse?

2. What should you do instead of starting an argument?

PARENT CHAT:

When our feelings are hurt or we begin to get angry with someone, it's hard to do the right thing. Talk with your parents and ask them for suggestions about how to be a peacemaker — someone who brings about peace, especially reconciling adversaries or helping someone work out their problems in a gentle way. Make a list of three things you can do or say to someone instead of arguing with them when a problem arises.

DAY 10

💬 **TODAY'S VERSE: PROVERBS 19:11 (NIV)**

A person's wisdom yields patience;
   it is to one's glory to overlook an offense.

⭐ **COPY THE VERSE HERE:**

➡ **BIG IDEA:**

Wise people are patient!

♡KID CORNER:

1. What does a person's wisdom or good sense do?

2. What should we do when someone offends us?

💬PARENT CHAT:

It's a challenge to be patient, even for your mom and dad! Think for a minute about what makes it hard for you to be patient. Then, fill in the blanks:

I am most patient when _____.

I have a hard time being patient when _____.

Next, ask your parents to tell you what comes to their mind when they think about the word "patience."

DAY 11

🗨 **TODAY'S VERSE: PROVERBS 20:22 (NIV)**

Do not say, "I'll pay you back for this wrong!"
Wait for the Lord, and He will avenge you.

⭐ **COPY THE VERSE HERE:**

➟ **BIG IDEA:**

Do not get back at others!

♡KID CORNER:

1. What should we never say?

2. If we wait for the Lord, what will He do?

■PARENT CHAT:

Jesus died on the cross for the sin of the world — including all your sins and your parents' sins. When He was on trial before He died, people were mean to Him and called Him terrible names. He remained silent as people accused Him of wrongdoing, even though He was innocent. He even prayed on the cross and asked His Father to forgive them!

Talk about this with your parents: how does it feel to know that Jesus chose to die for you instead of punishing you for your sins? Is there someone you can show love to even though they may not treat you very well, just like Jesus did on the cross? It takes a strong person to let God handle those who hurt us instead of taking revenge, but God will always give us the strength we need when we ask! Take a moment and pray with your parents. Ask God to help you to never repay evil with evil!

DAY 12

TODAY'S VERSE: PROVERBS 12:10 (NIV)

The righteous care for the needs of their animals, but the kindest acts of the wicked are cruel.

★COPY THE VERSE HERE:

BIG IDEA:

Take good care of animals!

♡ KID CORNER:

1. What do righteous or good people do?

2. What word describes the actions of wicked people?

🗨 PARENT CHAT:

Do you have a pet, or animals on your land? How about in your neighborhood or classroom? Are you responsible for helping to take care of them? Talk to your parents about the job you are doing and be open to their advice about improving. Parents, be sure to praise your child for a job well done! Whether you have your own animals or not, discuss something you can do in the next week to show kindness to an animal — like spending some time at an animal rescue shelter to pet the animals and show them affection, or leaving out a water bowl in front of your home for dogs who are out on walks with their owner!

DAY 13

💬TODAY'S VERSE: PROVERBS 22:1 (NIV)

A good name is more desirable than great riches;
to be esteemed is better than silver or gold.

⭐COPY THE VERSE HERE:

→BIG IDEA:

What others think about you is important!

♥KID CORNER:

1. What is better than riches or money?

2. What is more valuable than silver or gold?

PARENT CHAT:

Even though not everyone will like us all the time, we should want a good reputation with others. Talk with your parents and ask them what three words describe you best. Then, ask them to be honest with you and talk about one of your weaknesses that might hurt your good name. Talk about ways you can build up your reputation at home, school, and other places! Now it's your turn — do the same thing for your mom or dad so they can grow in wisdom, too!

DAY 14

TODAY'S VERSE: PROVERBS 25:28 (NIV)

Like a city whose walls are broken through
is a person who lacks self-control.

★ **COPY THE VERSE HERE:**

BIG IDEA:

Be self-controlled!

♥ KID CORNER:

1. What is a person without self-control like?

2. What's the problem with this kind of city or house?

💬 PARENT CHAT:

Try this: take turns making up a story together about a boy or girl who didn't have self-control. What is your character's name? Where do they live? In what area do they have trouble with self-control? Is it with food or candy? Fighting with siblings? Playing instead of doing homework? What happens in the end? Does your story have a happy ending or a sad one?

DAY 15

TODAY'S VERSE: PRVERBS 26:17 (ESV)

Whoever meddles in a quarrel not his own
is like one who takes a passing dog by the ears.

★ COPY THE VERSE HERE:

→ BIG IDEA:

Don't join an argument!

♥KID CORNER:

1. Describe someone who meddles in a quarrel.

2. What could happen to you if you interfere in someone else's argument?

▨PARENT CHAT:

Sometimes, we want to help others, so we jump into their argument. Just as aggravating a stray or dangerous dog is a bad idea, so is getting involved in someone else's fight. But maybe there is a better way to help. Together with your parents, list three things you can do that are honorable and wise if someone else is having a problem with another person, instead of entering into the fight yourself.

DAY 16

TODAY'S VERSE: PROVERBS 20:19 (NIV)

A gossip betrays a confidence,
    so avoid anyone who talks too much.

★ COPY THE VERSE HERE:

BIG IDEA:

Don't be friends with a gossip!

♡KID CORNER:

1. What does a gossip do?

2. Who should we avoid?

PARENT CHAT:

To gossip means to say things about someone that are private, or to say mean or untrue things about others. Gossips often say these things to try and make themselves look good by putting others down secretly. Let's do just the opposite, shall we? Ask your parents to provide some paper you can fold in half to make a note or use some cards you already have. Choose someone you know and write a short note to them, telling them something you like or appreciate about them. Be sure to hand it to them, or mail it this week! Instead of spreading unkind information behind someone's back, talking to them directly and saying something to encourage them is a wise thing to do!

DAY 17

TODAY'S VERSE: PROVERBS 19:17 (NIV)

Whoever is kind to the poor lends to the Lord,
and He will reward them for what they have done.

★ COPY THE VERSE HERE:

→ BIG IDEA:

Take care of the poor!

♡ KID CORNER:

1. When we give to the poor, who are we really giving to?

2. What will the Lord do for us when we are generous to those in need?

💬 PARENT CHAT:

There are people in need all around us. Some people live on the streets without homes of their own; others may have shelter, but lack things that they need, like school supplies or warm clothes. Many organizations welcome volunteers to help pack food boxes or serve meals. Brainstorm some ideas with your parents about ways you can help someone in need. Choose to act as soon as possible and give generously of your time or resources to others. Then, look for the ways that God rewards you for your generosity and thank Him for providing for your needs too.

DAY 18

TODAY'S VERSE: PROVERBS 30:5 (NIV)

Every word of God is flawless;

He is a shield to those who take refuge in Him.

★ **COPY THE VERSE HERE:**

BIG IDEA:

The Bible is true!

♥ KID CORNER:

1. What does this verse tell us about the Word of God?

2. God is a shield for whom?

💬 PARENT CHAT:

We can trust God's Word to be true and right. This gives us peace and comfort, knowing we can believe God. In this verse, God promises to protect us when we go to Him! Is there something that you feel scared or nervous about? Talk about it with your mom or dad. Then, pray together, asking for God's help and protection. Know that God will be with you and help you!

DAY 19

TODAY'S VERSE: PROVERBS 18:2 (NIV)

Fools find no pleasure in understanding
but delight in airing their own opinions.

★ COPY THE VERSE HERE:

➔ BIG IDEA:

Listen to other people's opinions!

♡KID CORNER:

1. What kind of person avoids understanding the thoughts or ideas of others?

2. According to this verse, what does a fool like to do?

💬PARENT CHAT:

It's okay to have a conversation with someone and each share your opinions, but the foolish person is more concerned about themselves than what their friend is saying. Let's practice listening to the thoughts and ideas of others. Ask your parents one of the following questions and don't interrupt them! Listen carefully and don't try to talk about your own opinions! Then, simply tell them that their answers were interesting!

Questions:

- What is your idea of a perfect vacation?
- Which do you like more: fall, winter, spring, or summer? Why?
- Would you rather live in a tree house or in an underground cave? Why?

DAY 20

💬TODAY'S VERSE: PROVERBS 6:20-21 (NIV)

My son, keep your father's command
    and do not forsake your mother's teaching.
Bind them always on your heart;
    fasten them around your neck.

★COPY THE VERSE HERE:

BIG IDEA:

Obey your parents!

♥KID CORNER:

1. Whose commands and teachings should you obey?

2. Where should you bind or fasten them?

▣PARENT CHAT:

As children, God tells us to obey our parents! He compares their commands to putting on clothes. Getting dressed is something we do every day. Our obedience to our parents should be an everyday act, too. Is there something that your parents have to ask you to do often, but you don't listen? Or is there something they have to ask you to stop doing? If you want your life to be a happy one that is full of good things, then listening to your parents is important. Talk to them now and ask them how you can obey better this week. Then, commit to do what they ask you to do!

WRAP UP:

Look at you! It's obvious that you are a much wiser kid now than when you first started your Study Buddy Bible Study in Proverbs! Remember that following God's Word is for your benefit and it gives God the glory and honor He deserves.

Here's one final challenge for you! Go back and choose one Bible verse to memorize. Invite mom or dad to memorize it with you! Write it out and put it on display somewhere in your home and be sure to do what it says.

Congratulations on a job well done! Let's continue to apply what we have learned in the book of Proverbs, today and every day!

ABOUT THE AUTHOR:

A former high school English teacher, Amber Lia is a work-at-home mom of four little boys under the age of ten. She and her husband, Guy, own Storehouse Media Group, a faith- and family-friendly TV and Film production company in Los Angeles, CA. When she's not building sand castles with her boys on the beach, or searching for Nerf darts all over her house, you can find Amber writing to encourage families on her blog at Mother of Knights (www.motherofknights.com). And be sure to check out her first book, Triggers: Exchanging Parents' Angry Reactions for Gentle Biblical Responses!

Made in the USA
Lexington, KY
30 May 2017